Ultimate Chromebook Bible

The Essential A-Z
Handbook for Everyone

Jerry P. G. Bill

TABLE OF CONTENTS

Ultimate Chromebook Bible

Introduction

Welcome to the world of Chromebooks! These sleek, efficient devices have transformed the way we work, learn, and play by offering a simple, streamlined computing experience. Whether you're looking to browse the web, complete school assignments, manage professional tasks, or simply enjoy multimedia entertainment, a Chromebook can handle it all with ease.

Unlike traditional laptops, Chromebooks are built around Google's ChromeOS, a cloud-first operating system that emphasizes speed, security, and simplicity. From lightning-fast boot times to seamless integration with Google services like Gmail, Google Drive, and Google Photos, Chromebooks are designed to make your life easier and more connected.

This guide is here to walk you through every aspect of owning and using a Chromebook, from getting started with your device to mastering advanced features. No matter your level of technical expertise, you'll find everything you need to become a confident Chromebook user.

What Makes Chromebooks Unique

Chromebooks stand out from traditional laptops and other computing devices due to their distinctive features and philosophy. Let's explore what makes them so special:

1. **Speed and Simplicity**
   Chromebooks are incredibly fast, with most devices booting up in under 10 seconds. The interface is clean and intuitive, making it easy for users of all skill levels to navigate. There's no need to worry about managing complex software installations or dealing with system slowdowns.

2. **Cloud-Centric Approach**

   ChromeOS is built around the idea of cloud computing. While Chromebooks have local storage, they thrive when connected to the internet, allowing users to store files, access apps, and back up data in the cloud. Google Drive integration ensures your files are always accessible from any device.

3. **Built-in Security**

   Chromebooks are known for their robust security features. Automatic updates, sandboxing, and built-in virus protection keep your device safe from threats without requiring additional software. ChromeOS also includes a verified boot process to ensure the system hasn't been tampered with.

4. **Affordable and Accessible**

   Chromebooks are typically more affordable than traditional laptops, offering excellent value for users who primarily rely on web-based applications. Their lower cost makes them an attractive option for students, families, and budget-conscious professionals.

5. **Diverse App Ecosystem**

   With access to both the Google Play Store and Chrome Web Store, Chromebooks offer a vast range of apps, from productivity tools to entertainment options. Whether you need Android apps or web-based solutions, Chromebooks provide flexibility and versatility.

6. **Seamless Integration with Google Services**

   Chromebooks are deeply integrated with Google's ecosystem. If you use Gmail, Google Calendar, Google Docs, or other Google services, you'll appreciate the seamless connection across your devices and accounts.

7. **Lightweight Design and Long Battery Life**

   Most Chromebooks are designed to be lightweight and portable, making them ideal for travel and on-the-go use. Additionally, their energy-efficient hardware ensures long battery life, often lasting 10 hours or more on a single charge.

8. **Frequent Updates and Future-Ready**

   Google regularly updates ChromeOS to introduce new features and improvements. These updates are automatic and free, ensuring your Chromebook stays current and capable.

Who This Guide Is For

This guide is designed for anyone who is new to Chromebooks, whether you've just purchased your first device or are considering making the switch. Here's a breakdown of who will benefit most:

1. **First-Time Chromebook Users**
   If you're unfamiliar with ChromeOS or are transitioning from a Windows or Mac computer, this guide will help you get up to speed quickly and confidently.

2. **Students and Educators**
   Chromebooks are a favorite in educational settings due to their affordability, simplicity, and collaborative tools. Students will find tips for staying organized, while educators will discover tools for managing classrooms and enhancing lessons.

3. **Professionals and Remote Workers**
   For professionals looking to streamline their workflow or work remotely, Chromebooks offer a secure, cloud-based platform. This guide covers productivity tips, app recommendations, and strategies for optimizing your work environment.

4. **Budget-Conscious Shoppers**

   If you're seeking a cost-effective alternative to traditional laptops, Chromebooks are an excellent choice. This guide will help you make the most of your investment by exploring features, apps, and accessories that enhance your experience.

5. **Tech Enthusiasts and Tinkerers**

   ChromeOS isn't just for casual users. Advanced features like Linux app support and Developer Mode provide opportunities for tech enthusiasts to explore and experiment.

6. **Parents and Families**

   Chromebooks are an ideal choice for families, thanks to their child-friendly features, parental controls, and ability to manage multiple accounts on one device.

No matter your background, this guide will provide the knowledge and tools you need to make the most of your Chromebook. Let's dive in and unlock the full potential of your device!

Getting Started

Choosing the Right Chromebook for Your Needs

Before diving into the Chromebook experience, selecting the right device is crucial to ensure it meets your specific needs. Here are some factors to consider when choosing a Chromebook:

1. **Purpose and Usage**

   o **For Students**: Look for an affordable model with durability and long battery life. Features like a touchscreen and 2-in-1 design (laptop and tablet mode) are useful for note-taking and presentations.

- **For Professionals**: Opt for a Chromebook with higher processing power (Intel Core i5 or i7) and ample RAM (8GB or more) for multitasking and productivity. A larger display (13–15 inches) is also ideal for detailed work.
- **For Families**: A budget-friendly device with multiple user account support and built-in parental controls is ideal. Rugged models may be better suited for younger children.
- **For Creatives**: Seek out Chromebooks with high-resolution displays, stylus support, and robust Android app compatibility for tasks like photo editing and digital art.

2. **Performance Specifications**

- **Processor**: Entry-level models typically have Intel Celeron or

MediaTek processors, which are sufficient for web browsing and light tasks. For more demanding applications, look for Intel Core or AMD Ryzen processors.

- **RAM**: 4GB of RAM is standard for casual users, but 8GB or more is recommended for multitasking and running Android or Linux apps.
- **Storage**: Chromebooks rely on cloud storage, so local storage requirements are minimal. A 32GB or 64GB drive is usually sufficient, but 128GB is better for those who plan to store media or install numerous apps.

3. **Display and Size**

- Smaller screens (11–12 inches) are portable and lightweight, while larger displays (14–15 inches) provide better viewing and workspace. Consider resolution; Full HD (1080p) or higher is recommended for a sharp, clear image.

4. **Battery Life**

   ○ Chromebooks are known for their long battery life. Look for models offering 10 hours or more to ensure all-day use.

5. **Special Features**

   ○ **Touchscreen and 2-in-1 Design**: These are great for versatility, especially if you use Android apps or prefer tablet mode.
   ○ **Stylus Support**: Essential for creatives and note-takers.
   ○ **Ports and Connectivity**: Check for USB-C, USB-A, headphone jacks, and microSD slots. Bluetooth and Wi-Fi 6 are also advantageous.

6. **Budget**

   ○ Chromebooks range from budget-friendly models under $300

to premium devices costing over $1,000. Assess your needs to avoid overpaying for unnecessary features.

Unboxing and Initial Setup

Opening a new Chromebook is an exciting moment! Follow these steps for a smooth start:

1. **Unbox Your Device**

    ○ Carefully unpack the Chromebook, charging adapter, and any included accessories.
    ○ Inspect the device for any visible damage during shipping.

2. **Charge the Battery**

    ○ Connect the Chromebook to its charger and plug it into a power outlet. Although most devices arrive partially charged, it's good practice to fully charge the battery before initial use.

3. **Power On the Device**

   ○ Press the power button (usually located at the top-right corner of the keyboard or on the side of the device).

4. **Select Your Language and Region**

   ○ Upon starting, you'll be prompted to choose your preferred language, keyboard layout, and region.

5. **Connect to Wi-Fi**

   ○ Select your Wi-Fi network from the list and enter the password. A stable internet connection is essential for setup.

6. **Review the Terms of Service**

   ○ Read and accept Google's Terms of Service to proceed.

Signing In with a Google Account

To unlock the full potential of your Chromebook, you'll need to sign in with a Google account:

1. **Sign In with an Existing Account**

   o Enter your Google account email address and password. If you use Gmail, Google Drive, or other Google services, this is your Google account.

2. **Create a New Account (if needed)**

   o If you don't already have a Google account, select "Create Account" and follow the steps to set up a new one.

3. **Sync Settings**

   o Once signed in, you'll have the option to sync settings, bookmarks, and preferences from other devices linked to your account. This ensures a seamless experience across devices.

4. **Enable or Skip Google Assistant**

   ○ You'll be prompted to set up Google Assistant. Enabling it allows for voice commands and smart assistant features.

5. **Set Up Parental Controls (if applicable)**

   ○ For child accounts, parents can configure supervision through Google Family Link, ensuring a safe browsing experience.

Exploring the ChromeOS Interface

Once you've signed in, it's time to familiarize yourself with the ChromeOS interface:

1. **The Desktop**

   ○ The desktop is clean and minimalist, featuring a wallpaper

and a bottom toolbar called the
Shelf.

2. **The Shelf**

  ○ Located at the bottom of the screen,
  the Shelf acts as your app launcher
  and quick-access bar. It includes:
  - **App Icons**: Commonly used
    apps like Chrome, Gmail,
    and Google Docs.
  - **Launcher Button**: A circle
    icon that opens the app
    drawer, where you can find
    and search for apps.
  - **System Tray**: On the right
    side of the Shelf, it displays
    the clock, battery status, and
    quick settings like Wi-Fi and
    volume.

3. **App Drawer**

  ○ Accessed via the Launcher button,
  the app drawer displays all installed

apps. You can organize or search for apps here.

4. **Files App**

   o This is the file manager for ChromeOS, allowing you to access downloads, local storage, Google Drive, and connected devices.

5. **Quick Settings Menu**

   o Found in the bottom-right corner of the Shelf, this menu includes Wi-Fi, Bluetooth, volume, and other quick-access settings.

6. **Navigating with the Touchpad**

   o Master touchpad gestures for efficient navigation:
      ▪ **Single Tap**: Left-click
      ▪ **Two-Finger Tap**: Right-click
      ▪ **Two-Finger Scroll**: Move up or down pages
      ▪ **Three-Finger Swipe**: Switch between tabs

Understanding ChromeOS

ChromeOS is the lightweight, cloud-centric operating system powering Chromebooks. Built by Google, it's designed for speed, simplicity, and security. This section will explain the key features of ChromeOS, help you navigate the interface, and guide you through some of its most powerful tools.

Key Features of ChromeOS

1. **Fast and Lightweight**

○ ChromeOS is optimized for speed, allowing Chromebooks to boot up in seconds. The system uses minimal resources, ensuring smooth performance even on lower-spec devices.

2. **Cloud-Centric Design**

○ ChromeOS emphasizes cloud storage, with seamless integration with Google Drive. While local storage is available, most tasks, such as file saving and app usage, are performed in the cloud.

3. **Google Ecosystem Integration**

○ ChromeOS integrates deeply with Google services like Gmail, Google Docs, Google Photos, and Google Calendar. This connectivity allows you to access your files and settings from any device.

4. **Automatic Updates**

○ ChromeOS updates itself in the
background, ensuring you always
have the latest features and security
patches without manual
intervention.

5. **Built-In Security**

○ ChromeOS includes multiple layers
of security, such as sandboxing,
verified boot, and automatic
malware protection, making
Chromebooks one of the safest
platforms.

6. **Support for Android and Linux Apps**

○ In addition to web apps, ChromeOS
supports Android apps from the
Google Play Store and Linux
applications, providing a versatile
software ecosystem.

7. **Offline Functionality**

○ While ChromeOS thrives online,
many apps, including Google Docs,

Gmail, and more, offer offline modes so you can stay productive even without an internet connection.

8. **User-Friendly Design**

   ○ ChromeOS is intuitive and straightforward, with a clean interface that minimizes distractions and maximizes productivity.

The App Launcher and Shelf

The App Launcher and Shelf are central to navigating ChromeOS. Here's how they work:

1. **The Shelf**

   ○ The Shelf is the taskbar-like strip at the bottom of the screen, providing quick access to frequently used apps and settings.

- ○ **Pinned Apps**: You can pin your favorite apps for one-click access. Right-click an app and select "Pin to Shelf."
- ○ **Status Area**: Located on the right, it shows the clock, battery, Wi-Fi status, and quick settings.

2. **The App Launcher**

- ○ The App Launcher (the circle icon on the far left of the Shelf) is your gateway to all apps. Click it to open a search bar and a grid of installed apps.
- ○ **Search Bar**: Type here to search your apps, files, and even the web directly.
- ○ **Organizing Apps**: Drag and drop apps to reorder them in the grid or group them into folders for easier access.

3. **Quick Access Features**

○ You can access Google Assistant directly from the App Launcher, allowing you to perform voice commands or searches.

Navigating with the Touchpad and Touchscreen

Navigating ChromeOS efficiently is key to getting the most out of your Chromebook. ChromeOS offers intuitive gestures and touch controls:

1. **Touchpad Gestures**

   ○ **Single Tap**: Equivalent to a left-click.
   ○ **Double Tap**: Selects text or items.
   ○ **Two-Finger Tap**: Opens the right-click menu.
   ○ **Two-Finger Scroll**: Drag two fingers vertically or horizontally to scroll through pages or lists.

○ **Pinch to Zoom**: Use two fingers to zoom in or out on a webpage or document.

○ **Three-Finger Swipe**:

■ Swipe up: Opens the Overview mode, displaying all open windows.

■ Swipe left or right: Switches between open tabs in the Chrome browser.

2. **Touchscreen Gestures (on touchscreen-enabled Chromebooks)**

○ **Tap**: Selects an item.

○ **Swipe Down**: Refreshes a page or pulls down menus.

○ **Pinch to Zoom**: Works similarly to the touchpad.

○ **Swipe Left or Right**: Navigates back and forth in apps or the browser.

3. **Keyboard Shortcuts**

- ○ ChromeOS has extensive shortcuts to boost productivity. For example:
  - ■ **Ctrl + Shift + T**: Reopens the last closed tab.
  - ■ **Ctrl + Window Switcher Key**: Takes a screenshot.

Using Multiple Desktops (Virtual Desks)

Virtual Desks, a powerful feature of ChromeOS, allow you to organize your workspace and multitask more effectively:

1. **What Are Virtual Desks?**

   - ○ Virtual Desks create separate desktop environments, letting you group apps and windows by task. For example, you could have one desk for work, one for personal browsing, and another for entertainment.

2. **Creating and Managing Virtual Desks**

- **Create a New Desk**:
  - Open Overview Mode by swiping up with three fingers on the touchpad or pressing **Search + =**.
  - Click the "+ New Desk" button at the top of the screen.
- **Switch Between Desks**:
  - Swipe left or right with four fingers on the touchpad, or select a desk in Overview Mode.
- **Move Windows Between Desks**:
  - Drag a window to a different desk in Overview Mode.

3. **Use Cases for Virtual Desks**

- **Work and Personal Separation**: Keep work-related apps like Google Docs and Zoom on one desk while personal tabs like social media are on another.

○ **Project Organization**: Dedicate desks to specific projects or tasks to avoid clutter and distraction.

○ **Entertainment and Leisure**: Set up a desk for streaming video or playing games.

4. **Closing a Desk**

○ To close a desk, go to Overview Mode and click the "X" on the desk you want to remove. Open windows from that desk will automatically move to another active desk.

Connecting to the Internet and Devices

One of the key strengths of Chromebooks is their connectivity, making it simple to access the internet and integrate with other devices. In this section, we'll walk through how to connect your Chromebook to the internet, pair peripherals using Bluetooth, connect external monitors, and set up printing.

Wi-Fi and Ethernet Setup

Connecting to the internet is fundamental to using your Chromebook, as ChromeOS is a cloud-based operating system.

Wi-Fi Setup

1. **Accessing Wi-Fi Settings**:

   o Click on the **Status Area** in the bottom-right corner of the screen (where the clock and battery icon are displayed).
   o Select the Wi-Fi icon to view available networks.

2. **Connecting to a Wi-Fi Network**:

   o Choose your network from the list of available connections.
   o Enter the network password when prompted and click **Connect**.
   o Once connected, a Wi-Fi symbol will appear in the Status Area.

3. **Connecting to a Hidden Network**:

   o If your network does not appear in the list, click **Join Other Network**.

○ Enter the network name (SSID),
   security type, and password to
   connect.

Ethernet Setup

1. **Using an Ethernet Adapter**:

   ○ Chromebooks don't usually have
      built-in Ethernet ports, so you'll
      need a USB-to-Ethernet or
      USB-C-to-Ethernet adapter.
   ○ Plug the adapter into your
      Chromebook and connect it to an
      Ethernet cable.

2. **Automatic Connection**:

   ○ ChromeOS will automatically
      detect the Ethernet connection and
      connect to the network.
   ○ You can confirm the connection in
      the Status Area, where a wired
      network icon will appear.

Bluetooth Pairing for Peripherals

Chromebooks support Bluetooth for connecting peripherals like mice, keyboards, headphones, and speakers.

1. **Accessing Bluetooth Settings**:

   ○ Click the **Status Area** and select the Bluetooth icon. If Bluetooth is off, toggle it on.

2. **Pairing a Device**:

   ○ Ensure the device you want to connect is in pairing mode.
   ○ On your Chromebook, click **Pair New Device** to see a list of available devices.
   ○ Select your device from the list and follow any on-screen instructions to complete the pairing process.

3. **Managing Paired Devices**:

○ Once paired, your device will automatically reconnect when in range.
○ To disconnect or remove a device, click the device name in the Bluetooth settings and select **Disconnect** or **Remove Device**.

Connecting External Monitors

Chromebooks allow you to connect external monitors for extended screen real estate, which is especially useful for multitasking or presentations.

1. **Compatible Ports and Adapters**:

○ Most Chromebooks feature HDMI, USB-C, or DisplayPort outputs. Use the appropriate cable or adapter for your external monitor.
○ For USB-C, ensure your cable supports video output.

2. **Connecting the Monitor**:

   ○ Plug the monitor into your
     Chromebook using the appropriate
     cable.
   ○ ChromeOS will automatically
     detect the monitor and extend the
     display.

3. **Adjusting Display Settings**:

   ○ Open **Settings** > **Device** >
     Displays.
   ○ Here, you can:
       ▪ Adjust resolution and
         orientation.
       ▪ Choose to extend the screen
         or mirror the Chromebook
         display.
       ▪ Set which screen is the
         primary display.

4. **Using a Docking Station**:

   ○ If you have multiple monitors or
     additional peripherals, consider

using a USB-C docking station to streamline connections.

Printing from a Chromebook

Although Chromebooks don't traditionally support direct printer drivers, they offer seamless printing options through network-connected or cloud-compatible printers.

1. **Using a Wi-Fi Printer**:

   - Ensure your printer is connected to the same Wi-Fi network as your Chromebook.
   - Open **Settings** > **Advanced** > **Printing** > **Printers**.
   - Click **Add Printer**, and ChromeOS will search for available printers.
   - Select your printer and click **Add** to complete the setup.

2. **Using a USB Printer**:

- ○ Connect the printer to your Chromebook using a USB cable.
- ○ ChromeOS will automatically detect the printer and add it to your list of available printers.

3. **Printing a Document**:

- ○ Open the document or web page you want to print.
- ○ Press **Ctrl + P** or select **Print** from the menu.
- ○ Choose your printer from the dropdown list and adjust settings like page range, orientation, and copies.
- ○ Click **Print** to send the job to the printer.

4. **Printing Without a Compatible Printer**:

- ○ If your printer doesn't directly support ChromeOS, you can use Google Cloud Print alternatives, such as third-party apps (e.g., HP

Smart or Epson iPrint), which allow mobile printing from Chromebooks.

Chromebook Apps and Extensions

Chromebooks thrive on apps and extensions, offering a customizable experience tailored to your needs. From the Google Play Store to Chrome extensions, you have access to thousands of tools to enhance productivity, entertainment, and creativity.

Installing Apps from the Google Play Store

One of ChromeOS's standout features is its compatibility with Android apps from the Google Play Store. These apps provide expanded functionality beyond web-based applications.

1. **Enabling the Google Play Store**:

   ○ Most Chromebooks come with the Google Play Store enabled by default. If not, follow these steps:
      ■ Open **Settings** > **Apps** > **Google Play Store**.
      ■ Toggle on **Enable Google Play Store** and agree to the terms of service.

2. **Browsing the Play Store**:

   ○ Open the Play Store from the app launcher.
   ○ Use the search bar to find specific apps or browse categories such as productivity, games, and entertainment.

3. **Installing an App**:

   ○ Click on the app you want to install.
   ○ Select **Install**, and the app will be downloaded and added to your app drawer.

4. **Uninstalling Apps**:

   ○ To remove an app, right-click its
     icon in the app drawer or shelf and
     select **Uninstall**.

5. **Using Android Apps on a Chromebook**:

   ○ Android apps behave similarly to
     web apps. You can resize,
     minimize, and maximize app
     windows, and many apps support
     touchscreen gestures and offline
     use.

Using Chrome Extensions

Chrome extensions are lightweight add-ons that
enhance the functionality of the Chrome browser
and integrate seamlessly with ChromeOS.

1. **Accessing the Chrome Web Store**:

- Open the Chrome browser and navigate to the **Chrome Web Store** (accessible via a Google search or directly at https://chrome.google.com/webstore).

2. **Installing an Extension**:

- Browse or search for the desired extension.
- Click **Add to Chrome** and confirm the installation.
- The extension's icon will appear in the browser toolbar for quick access.

3. **Managing Extensions**:

- Open **Chrome Menu** > **More Tools** > **Extensions** to view and manage installed extensions.
- Here, you can enable/disable extensions, adjust permissions, or remove them entirely.

4. Best Practices for Extensions:

- Only install extensions from trusted developers to avoid performance or security issues.
- Keep extensions updated for compatibility and functionality.

Managing App Permissions

Managing app and extension permissions is critical for maintaining security and privacy. ChromeOS makes it easy to control which resources apps can access.

1. Adjusting App Permissions:

- Open **Settings** > **Apps**.
- Select the app or extension for which you want to modify permissions.

- Toggle options such as camera, microphone, location, and storage access based on your preferences.

2. **Reviewing Permissions Regularly**:

   - Periodically review permissions to ensure apps and extensions aren't accessing unnecessary or sensitive data.

3. **Revoking Permissions**:

   - If an app or extension no longer requires certain permissions, you can revoke them in the settings or uninstall the app entirely.

4. **Parental Controls**:

   - For child accounts, use **Google Family Link** to monitor and limit app permissions.

Top Apps and Extensions for Productivity

Maximizing your Chromebook's potential involves selecting the right apps and extensions. Here are some top recommendations across various categories:

1. Productivity Apps

- **Google Workspace (Docs, Sheets, Slides)**: Essential tools for document creation, spreadsheets, and presentations.
- **Trello**: A powerful app for project management and task tracking.
- **Grammarly**: A Chrome extension that helps improve your writing by catching grammar and spelling errors.
- **Notion**: A versatile app for note-taking, task management, and collaboration.

2. Communication and Collaboration

- **Zoom**: For video conferencing and virtual meetings.
- **Slack**: A widely used tool for team communication and collaboration.

- **Google Meet**: A seamless option for video calls integrated into Google Workspace.

3. File Management

- **Files by Google**: Efficient file organization and management.
- **Solid Explorer**: A robust file manager with cloud integration.

4. Creative Tools

- **Canva**: An intuitive design tool for creating graphics, presentations, and social media posts.
- **Adobe Lightroom**: For photo editing and image enhancements.
- **Krita**: A digital art app compatible with Chromebooks.

5. Browser Extensions

- **LastPass**: A password manager for secure and convenient access to accounts.

- **Pocket**: Save articles and web pages to read later.
- **Honey**: Automatically applies coupon codes for online shopping.
- **Tab Wrangler**: Manages inactive tabs to optimize browser performance.

6. Entertainment and Leisure

- **Spotify**: Stream music and create playlists.
- **Netflix**: Enjoy movies and TV shows offline with the app's download feature.
- **Google Play Books**: Access ebooks and audiobooks.

7. Coding and Development

- **Visual Studio Code**: A versatile code editor for developers.
- **Caret**: A text editor designed for coding in ChromeOS.
- **Linux Apps**: Use Linux-based development tools like Vim, Git, and Docker.

8. Education and Learning

- **Khan Academy**: Access free courses and tutorials on a variety of topics.
- **Duolingo**: Learn new languages interactively.
- **Quizlet**: Study and prepare for exams with flashcards and quizzes.

Web Browsing with Chrome

The Google Chrome browser is at the heart of the Chromebook experience, offering a fast, intuitive, and feature-rich platform for all your web browsing needs. ChromeOS is optimized for Chrome, making it the perfect tool for everything from casual browsing to professional productivity.

Mastering the Google Chrome Browser

The Chrome browser is designed for simplicity and speed, with powerful features that enhance productivity and convenience.

1. **Getting Started with Chrome**:

   ○ The browser is pre-installed on your Chromebook and opens automatically when you click the Chrome icon on the Shelf or in the Launcher.

2. **User-Friendly Interface**:

   ○ **Omnibox (Address Bar)**: This multipurpose bar allows you to type URLs, search queries, and even perform calculations or translations directly.

   ○ **Tabs**: Manage multiple webpages in a single window using tabs.

   ○ **Menu**: Access Chrome's settings, history, downloads, and extensions by clicking the three-dot menu in the top-right corner.

3. **Built-in Features**:

- o **Google Search Integration**: Seamless search powered by Google with personalized results.
- o **PDF Viewer**: View, annotate, and save PDFs directly in the browser.
- o **Translate**: Automatically translate web pages in foreign languages.

4. **Shortcuts to Save Time**:

- o **Ctrl + T**: Open a new tab.
- o **Ctrl + Shift + T**: Reopen the last closed tab.
- o **Ctrl + W**: Close the current tab.
- o **Alt + D**: Highlight the Omnibox.

Using Tabs and Bookmarks Efficiently

Managing tabs and bookmarks effectively can significantly enhance your browsing experience.

1. **Tabs**:

- o **Opening and Organizing Tabs**:

- Open new tabs with **Ctrl + T** or click the "+" icon at the top of the browser.
- Drag tabs to rearrange their order.
- Group related tabs together by right-clicking a tab and selecting **Add Tab to Group**. Name the group and assign a color for better organization.

○ **Pin Tabs**:

- Pin frequently used tabs (e.g., email or calendar) by right-clicking the tab and selecting **Pin Tab**. Pinned tabs are smaller and stay fixed on the left side of the tab bar.

○ **Tab Search**:

- Use the drop-down arrow in the top-right corner to search through open tabs quickly.

2. **Bookmarks**:

- ○ **Creating and Organizing Bookmarks**:
  - ■ Bookmark a page by clicking the star icon in the Omnibox or pressing **Ctrl + D**.
  - ■ Organize bookmarks into folders via the **Bookmarks Bar** or the **Bookmarks Manager** (accessible from the three-dot menu).
- ○ **Syncing Bookmarks**:
  - ■ If syncing is enabled, bookmarks are saved to your Google account and accessible on all devices where you're signed in.

3. **Quick Access Tips**:

- ○ Use the **Bookmarks Bar** for one-click access to frequently visited sites. Toggle it on/off with **Ctrl + Shift + B**.
- ○ Save time by bookmarking complex searches or frequently used tools.

Syncing Across Devices

One of Chrome's greatest advantages is its ability to sync data across devices, ensuring seamless transitions between your Chromebook, smartphone, tablet, or other computers.

1. **Enabling Sync**:

   o Sign in to Chrome with your Google account to enable sync.
   o Open **Settings** > **You and Google** > **Sync and Google Services**.

2. **What Sync Covers**:

   o Sync can include bookmarks, history, passwords, open tabs, extensions, and settings. You can customize what to sync by selecting **Manage What You Sync**.

3. **Accessing Synced Data**:

- ○ Open Chrome on another device and sign in with the same Google account to access your bookmarks, saved passwords, and browsing history instantly.
- ○ Use **Tabs from Other Devices** in the History menu to continue browsing from where you left off.

4. **Security Measures**:

- ○ Enable **Encryption for Synced Data** in the settings for added privacy. You can use your Google account credentials or create a custom passphrase for encryption.

Privacy and Security Settings

Chrome provides robust tools to protect your privacy and ensure secure browsing.

1. **Customizing Privacy Settings**:

- Open **Settings** > **Privacy and Security** to manage various options.
  - **Clear Browsing Data**: Remove cookies, cached files, or browsing history.
  - **Do Not Track**: Enable this option to request websites not to track your online activity.

2. **Secure Browsing with Safe Browsing**:

- Chrome includes Safe Browsing, which warns you about potentially harmful websites, downloads, and extensions.
- You can enable Enhanced Protection for more proactive security measures.

3. **Managing Cookies and Site Data**:

- Control how websites use cookies by going to **Settings** > **Privacy and Security** > **Cookies and Other Site Data**. Options include blocking third-party cookies or clearing data after each session.

4. **Password Management**:

- Chrome has a built-in password manager that securely saves and autofills login credentials.
- Access it through **Settings** > **Autofill** > **Passwords**.
- Use the **Password Checkup** feature to identify weak or compromised passwords.

5. **Extensions and Permissions**:

- Regularly review installed extensions to ensure they come from trusted sources and don't overstep their permissions.
- Go to **Settings** > **Extensions** to manage or remove them.

6. **Incognito Mode**:

- Browse privately by opening a new Incognito window (**Ctrl** + **Shift** +

N). Incognito mode doesn't save your browsing history or cookies.

7. **Using a VPN for Extra Security**:

   ○ If privacy is a priority, consider using a VPN extension or app to encrypt your internet connection and mask your location.

File Management on Chromebook

Chromebooks offer a streamlined approach to file management, leveraging the cloud-first nature of ChromeOS while providing robust tools for local and external storage. In this section, we'll cover the basics of the **Files app**, managing files with Google Drive, using external drives and USBs, and handling file compression and sharing.

Understanding the Files App

The **Files app** on ChromeOS is your central hub for accessing and managing files, whether they're stored locally, in the cloud, or on external drives.

1. **Accessing the Files App**:

   o Click the **Launcher** (the circle icon in the bottom-left corner of your screen) and search for "Files," or locate it directly in the app drawer.
   o The app opens with a sidebar on the left for navigation and a main pane for file browsing.

2. **File Organization**:

   o The sidebar includes:
     ▪ **My Files**: Local files stored on your Chromebook.
     ▪ **Google Drive**: Files synced with your Google Drive account.
     ▪ **Recent**: A quick-access folder showing recently used files.

- **Audio/Images/Videos**: Automatically categorized media files.
- **Trash**: A recovery folder for deleted files (files in Trash are automatically deleted after 30 days).

3. **Creating and Managing Folders**:

  o To create a new folder:
    - Navigate to the location (e.g., My Files).
    - Right-click (or tap with two fingers on the touchpad) and select **New Folder**.
  o Rename, delete, or move files and folders using the same right-click menu or drag-and-drop functionality.

4. **Search Functionality**:

  o Use the search bar at the top of the Files app to quickly locate specific files by name or type.

5. File Preview:

○ Select a file and press the spacebar
to open a preview window, or
double-click to open it in the
default application.

Managing Cloud Storage with Google Drive

Google Drive is tightly integrated with
ChromeOS, offering seamless access to your
cloud files.

1. Accessing Google Drive:

○ Open the Files app and click
Google Drive in the sidebar. Your
Drive folders and files will appear,
and any changes made are synced
in real-time.

2. Uploading Files to Google Drive:

- ○ Drag files from **My Files** or external storage into the **Google Drive** folder.
- ○ Right-click a file and choose **Move to** > **Google Drive**.

3. **Offline Access**:

- ○ To access Drive files offline:
  - Open the Google Drive folder in the Files app.
  - Right-click a file or folder and select **Available Offline**.
- ○ Offline files will sync automatically when you reconnect to the internet.

4. **Managing Storage**:

- ○ View your Google Drive storage by clicking the gear icon in the Files app and selecting **Drive Settings**.
- ○ Use Google's web interface to organize and clean up storage if needed.

5. **Using Multiple Google Accounts**:

○ If you have multiple accounts, you can add them by clicking your profile icon in the Files app and selecting **Add Another Account**.

Working with External Drives and USBs

Chromebooks support external storage devices such as USB drives, SD cards, and external hard drives, making it easy to transfer files.

1. **Connecting External Storage**:

   ○ Plug your device into the appropriate port (USB or SD card slot).
   ○ ChromeOS automatically detects the device, and it appears in the Files app sidebar under **Devices**.

2. **Accessing and Managing Files**:

   ○ Click the device name to view its contents.

o Drag files between the external drive and Chromebook storage as needed.

3. **Safely Ejecting Drives**:

o Before unplugging, eject the device by clicking the eject icon next to its name in the sidebar to prevent data corruption.

4. **File System Compatibility**:

o ChromeOS supports common file systems like FAT32 and exFAT.
o NTFS drives are supported in read-only mode. If you need write access, reformat the drive or use a compatible external app.

File Compression and Sharing

File compression and sharing are essential for organizing and transferring files, especially when dealing with large amounts of data.

1. **File Compression**:

   ○ ChromeOS supports creating and
   extracting ZIP files.
     ■ To compress files:
       ■ Select the files or
       folders in the Files
       app.
       ■ Right-click and choose
       Zip Selection. A ZIP
       file will be created in
       the same location.
     ■ To extract a ZIP file:
       ■ Double-click the ZIP
       file. A virtual folder
       opens, allowing you to
       copy the contents.

2. **File Sharing Options**:

   ○ **Using Google Drive**:
     ■ Share files directly from
     Drive by right-clicking the
     file and selecting **Share**.

- Enter the recipient's email address and adjust sharing permissions (e.g., view, comment, or edit).
  - **Email Attachments**:
    - Attach files to emails directly from the Files app by dragging them into your email client's compose window.
  - **Nearby Share**:
    - ChromeOS supports **Nearby Share**, allowing you to send files wirelessly to nearby Chromebooks or Android devices.
    - Enable Nearby Share in **Settings > Connected Devices**. Select the file, click **Share**, and choose **Nearby Share**.
3. **Cloud-Based Sharing Services**:

○ Use third-party platforms like Dropbox, OneDrive, or WeTransfer for additional sharing options. Install their web apps or extensions for easy access.

Productivity on Chromebook

Chromebooks are designed to help you stay productive, leveraging Google's ecosystem and supporting a wide range of apps and tools for professional, educational, and personal use. This section explores key productivity features, including Google Workspace apps, video conferencing tools, working with PDFs, and task management and calendar solutions.

Using Google Workspace (Docs, Sheets, Slides)

Google Workspace is the cornerstone of productivity on Chromebooks, offering powerful, cloud-based tools for creating and collaborating on documents, spreadsheets, and presentations.

1. **Google Docs (Word Processing)**:

   - **Creating Documents**:
     - Open Google Docs from the app launcher or directly in Chrome at docs.google.com.
     - Use pre-designed templates for resumes, reports, and letters, or start from a blank document.
   - **Collaboration Features**:
     - Share documents by clicking the **Share** button and entering collaborators' email addresses. Assign permissions such as **View**, **Comment**, or **Edit**.

- Use the **Comments** feature to leave feedback, and track changes with **Suggesting Mode**.
  - ○ **Offline Editing**:
    - Enable offline editing in Google Docs settings. This allows you to work on documents without an internet connection, syncing changes once you reconnect.

2. **Google Sheets (Spreadsheets)**:

   - ○ **Data Management and Analysis**:
     - Use Sheets for tasks such as budgeting, tracking progress, or analyzing data.
     - Built-in formulas and functions (like **SUM**, **VLOOKUP**, and **FILTER**) make calculations and data analysis easy.
   - ○ **Charts and Graphs**:

- Create visual representations of data with the chart tool. Customize the style, colors, and labels to suit your needs.
  - **Collaboration**:
    - Work with teams on shared spreadsheets, monitor changes in real time, and use the **Version History** feature to revert to earlier versions if needed.

3. **Google Slides (Presentations)**:

   - **Creating Engaging Presentations**:
     - Build presentations using themes and layouts, or customize designs with text, images, and animations.
   - **Integrations with Other Workspace Apps**:
     - Insert charts from Sheets or links to Docs directly into your slides for seamless integration.

- ○ **Presentation Modes**:
  - ■ Present slides directly from your Chromebook, use a clicker, or enable audience participation with the **Q&A** tool.

Video Conferencing with Google Meet and Zoom

Chromebooks make video conferencing simple and effective, supporting platforms like Google Meet and Zoom for virtual meetings and collaboration.

1. **Google Meet**:

   - ○ **Starting a Meeting**:
     - ■ Open Meet from the app launcher or at meet.google.com.

- Schedule meetings directly through Google Calendar or create instant meetings.
  - **Features**:
    - Share your screen to present documents or slides.
    - Use **Breakout Rooms** and **Polls** to engage participants in interactive sessions.
    - Turn on captions for real-time transcription.
  - **Integration with Google Workspace**:
    - Meet integrates seamlessly with Gmail, Calendar, and other Workspace tools, simplifying scheduling and collaboration.

2. **Zoom**:

  - **Installing and Using Zoom**:
    - Download Zoom from the Google Play Store.

- ■ Log in and join meetings using a meeting link or ID.
- ○ **Optimized Features for Chromebooks**:
  - ■ Zoom on Chromebooks supports virtual backgrounds, breakout rooms, and screen sharing.
- ○ **Tips for Smooth Video Calls**:
  - ■ Close unnecessary tabs and apps to optimize performance.
  - ■ Use a reliable internet connection to avoid disruptions.

Creating and Editing PDFs

PDFs are a widely used format for sharing documents. Chromebooks offer tools for viewing, creating, and editing PDFs, both natively and through third-party apps.

1. **Viewing PDFs**:

   ○ ChromeOS includes a built-in PDF viewer for reading and basic annotation. Open any PDF file by double-clicking it in the Files app.

2. **Annotating and Editing PDFs**:

   ○ **Built-in Tools**:
     ■ Use the PDF viewer's annotation tools to highlight text, add comments, or draw.
   ○ **Third-Party Apps**:
     ■ **Adobe Acrobat Reader**: Download from the Google Play Store for advanced PDF editing features, such as form filling and signing.
     ■ **Kami**: A web-based PDF editor that allows for collaboration, annotation, and integration with Google Drive.

3. **Creating PDFs**:

   ○ Use Google Docs to create a document and download it as a PDF by selecting **File > Download > PDF Document**.
   ○ Convert images or other file types to PDF using tools like Smallpdf or online converters.

Task Management and Calendar Apps

Staying organized is crucial for productivity, and Chromebooks provide various tools for managing tasks and schedules.

1. **Google Tasks**:

   ○ **Integrated with Google Workspace**:
      ■ Access Google Tasks directly in Gmail, Calendar, or the Google Tasks app.

- Create task lists, set due dates, and add subtasks.
  - ○ **Sync Across Devices**:
    - Tasks sync automatically with your Google account, making them accessible on all your devices.

2. **Google Calendar**:

   - ○ **Scheduling and Reminders**:
     - Use Calendar to schedule meetings, set reminders, and organize events.
     - Color-code calendars for work, personal, or shared events.
   - ○ **Integration with Apps**:
     - Calendar integrates with Google Meet for scheduling video calls and with Tasks to create deadlines for your to-dos.
   - ○ **Offline Access**:

■ Enable offline mode to view and manage events without an internet connection.

3. **Third-Party Task Management Apps**:

○ **Trello**: A visual project management tool that uses boards, lists, and cards to track tasks.

○ **Asana**: Ideal for team collaboration and task tracking.

○ **Notion**: A flexible tool for notes, tasks, and project management.

4. **Digital Note-Taking**:

○ Use apps like **Google Keep** or **Evernote** for quick note-taking and idea organization.

○ Sync notes with Google Drive for easy access and sharing.

Multimedia and Entertainment

Chromebooks offer a robust and versatile platform for enjoying multimedia content and gaming, thanks to their support for streaming services, photo and video editing tools, Android apps, and seamless connectivity with smart TVs.

Streaming Video and Music

Chromebooks are built for streaming, offering access to countless platforms for watching movies, TV shows, and listening to music.

1. **Video Streaming**:

- ○ **Popular Platforms**:
  - ■ Access services like Netflix, YouTube, Hulu, Disney+, Amazon Prime Video, and more directly through their web apps or Android apps from the Google Play Store.
- ○ **Optimized Playback**:
  - ■ ChromeOS is optimized for high-quality video playback. For the best experience, use a stable internet connection and ensure your Chromebook supports Full HD or 4K resolution if applicable.
- ○ **Offline Viewing**:
  - ■ Many services, like Netflix and Amazon Prime Video, allow offline downloads via their Android apps. This is particularly useful for traveling or areas with limited connectivity.

2. **Music Streaming**:

   ○ **Platforms and Apps**:
      - Stream music on Spotify,
        Apple Music, YouTube
        Music, or Amazon Music.
        Access them via the web or
        their dedicated Android apps.
   ○ **Offline Listening**:
      - Download playlists or albums
        for offline listening using
        Android apps if your
        subscription plan supports it.
   ○ **Sound Quality**:
      - Enhance your listening
        experience with quality
        headphones or external
        speakers. Pair Bluetooth
        devices for wireless
        convenience.

3. **Web-based Streaming**:

   ○ Chrome's browser supports
     streaming content directly from

websites, and many platforms offer
progressive web apps (PWAs) for
smoother integration.

Editing Photos and Videos

Chromebooks are increasingly capable of
handling photo and video editing, with powerful
web-based and Android tools.

1. **Photo Editing**:

   - **Built-in Tools**:
     - ChromeOS includes a basic
       image editor in the Gallery
       app, allowing for cropping,
       rotating, and adjusting
       brightness or contrast.
   - **Advanced Editing Apps**:
     - **Adobe Photoshop Express**:
       A lightweight Android app
       for advanced photo editing,

including filters, effects, and retouching.

- **Pixlr**: A free web-based editor with features for layering, color correction, and creative effects.

- **Canva**: Ideal for creating graphics, social media posts, and more. It offers both a web app and an Android app.

○ **Integration with Google Photos**:

- Google Photos allows you to organize, edit, and enhance your pictures. It offers tools for auto-enhancements, cropping, and applying filters.

2. **Video Editing**:

○ **Basic Editing**:

- Use Google Photos to trim or stabilize video clips.

○ **Advanced Tools**:

- **WeVideo**: A cloud-based video editor accessible via the Chrome browser. It supports transitions, audio tracks, and effects.
- **KineMaster**: An Android app for professional-grade video editing with multi-layer support, chroma key, and export options in 4K.
- **Clipchamp**: Available as a web app, it offers robust editing tools for creating polished videos.

3. **Tips for Editing on Chromebooks**:

   - **Optimize Performance**: Close unnecessary apps and tabs during editing to maximize performance.
   - **Cloud Storage**: Save and access large files through Google Drive or an external drive to conserve local storage space.

Using Android Games on Chromebook

Chromebooks are compatible with thousands of Android games, offering a range of casual and high-performance gaming experiences.

1. **Installing Games**:

   - Access the Google Play Store and browse games available for Chromebooks. Download and install games just like on an Android device.

2. **Popular Games**:

   - Play popular titles like **Minecraft, Among Us, Genshin Impact**, and **Call of Duty: Mobile**.
   - Enjoy casual games like **Candy Crush, Sudoku**, or word puzzles.

3. **Optimized Gaming**:

- o **Touchscreen Support**:
  Chromebooks with touchscreens
  offer an intuitive gaming experience
  for mobile-optimized games.
- o **Keyboard and Mouse**: Many
  games support keyboard and mouse
  input, providing a more immersive
  experience.
- o **Controller Support**: Pair a
  Bluetooth controller for
  console-like gaming. Most
  Chromebooks support controllers
  like Xbox or PlayStation via
  Bluetooth.

4. **Gaming Performance**:

- o **Cloud Gaming**: For graphically
  intensive games, use cloud gaming
  services like **NVIDIA GeForce
  NOW, Xbox Cloud Gaming**, or
  Google Stadia (if supported).
  These platforms stream games
  directly to your Chromebook

without requiring powerful local hardware.

- o **System Optimization**: Keep your Chromebook updated and close background apps to ensure smooth gameplay.

Connecting to Smart TVs

Chromebooks make it easy to share content with smart TVs for a larger screen experience.

1. **Wireless Casting**:

  - o **Using Chromecast**:
    - ■ Chromebooks are fully compatible with Google's Chromecast devices and Chromecast-enabled TVs.
    - ■ To cast:
      - ■ Open Chrome on your Chromebook.

- Click the three-dot menu in the top-right corner.
- Select **Cast**, choose your device, and share your screen, browser tab, or specific app.
   - **Casting Tips**:
     - Ensure your Chromebook and TV are on the same Wi-Fi network for seamless casting.
     - Use Chrome's settings to adjust casting quality if needed.

2. **HDMI Connection**:

   - For a wired connection, plug your Chromebook into the TV using an HDMI cable.
   - Use the **Settings** > **Display** menu to adjust screen mirroring or extended display options.

3. **Miracast and Other Protocols**:

   ○ While ChromeOS doesn't natively
     support Miracast, third-party apps
     may bridge compatibility with some
     smart TVs.

4. **Streaming Content**:

   ○ Apps like Netflix and YouTube
     allow direct casting of video
     content to smart TVs without
     sharing the entire screen.

5. **Enhancing the Experience**:

   ○ Use external speakers or soundbars
     for better audio.
   ○ Adjust display settings on your TV
     to match the resolution and aspect
     ratio of your Chromebook.

Customizing Your Chromebook

Chromebooks offer a range of customization options to make your device truly yours, whether it's the look and feel, functionality, or accessibility features. By tailoring your Chromebook to suit your preferences and needs, you can enhance both aesthetics and efficiency.

Changing Themes and Wallpaper

Personalizing your Chromebook's visual style is an easy way to make the device feel like your own.

1. **Changing the Wallpaper**:

   ○ **Using Default Options**:
      ■ Right-click on the desktop (two-finger tap on the touchpad) and select **Set wallpaper & style**.
      ■ Browse through Google's curated categories, such as landscapes, abstract art, and solid colors.
   ○ **Daily Refresh**:
      ■ Choose the **Daily refresh** option in a wallpaper category to have a new wallpaper each day automatically.
   ○ **Custom Wallpaper**:
      ■ Select **My images** to upload and set your own photos as wallpaper. Supported formats include JPEG and PNG.
2. **Dark Mode and Light Mode**:

- ○ Access the **Set wallpaper & style** menu to toggle between **Dark Mode** and **Light Mode**. Dark Mode can reduce eye strain and improve visibility in low-light environments.
- ○ Enable **Auto Mode** to switch themes based on the time of day.

3. **Customizing the Browser Theme**:

- ○ Open the Chrome Web Store and search for **Themes**.
- ○ Install a theme that changes the appearance of your browser tabs, address bar, and other elements. Popular themes range from minimalistic designs to colorful patterns.
- ○ To reset, go to **Settings** > **Appearance** and click **Reset to Default**.

Customizing the Shelf and Quick Settings

The Shelf and Quick Settings menu on a Chromebook provide shortcuts to your most-used apps and settings, and customizing them can streamline your workflow.

1. **Customizing the Shelf**:

   o **Pinning Apps**:
      ■ Open the app launcher, right-click (two-finger tap) on an app icon, and select **Pin to shelf**.
   o **Rearranging Apps**:
      ■ Click and drag app icons on the Shelf to reorder them based on your preferences.
   o **Auto-hide the Shelf**:
      ■ Right-click on the Shelf and select **Shelf position** > **Auto-hide shelf** to maximize screen space.
   o **Positioning the Shelf**:
      ■ Move the Shelf to the left, right, or bottom of the screen

by selecting **Shelf position** from the right-click menu.

2. **Quick Settings**:

   ○ **Accessing Quick Settings**:
      ■ Click the clock in the bottom-right corner to open the Quick Settings menu.
   ○ **Customizing Quick Settings**:
      ■ Quick Settings include toggles for Wi-Fi, Bluetooth, Night Light, and more.
      ■ Use the **Edit** (pencil) icon to add, remove, or reorder these toggles based on your needs.
   ○ **Personalized Profiles**:
      ■ Set up different profiles with unique quick settings for work, study, or leisure.

Accessibility Features

Chromebooks are equipped with a wide range of accessibility features to ensure usability for everyone, including those with disabilities or specific needs.

1. **Enabling Accessibility Features**:

   o Open **Settings > Advanced > Accessibility > Manage accessibility features**.
2. **Common Accessibility Tools**:

   o **Screen Reader (ChromeVox)**:
      ▪ A built-in screen reader that reads out text on the screen for visually impaired users. Enable it in the Accessibility settings.
   o **Magnifier**:
      ▪ Adjust the display size using the **Full-screen magnifier** or **Docked magnifier**.
   o **High Contrast Mode**:

- Enable high contrast mode to improve text visibility.
  - **Dictation**:
    - Use voice typing to dictate text in any input field.
  - **Keyboard and Mouse Customization**:
    - Adjust keyboard repeat rates, enable sticky keys, or use on-screen keyboards.
    - Change mouse cursor size, color, and speed for better visibility and control.

3. **Live Captions**:

  - Enable live captions to transcribe audio and video content in real time. This is particularly helpful for individuals who are deaf or hard of hearing.

4. **Other Features**:

  - **Automatic Clicks**: Simulate clicks by hovering over an item.

○ **Switch Access**: Control your Chromebook using external switches.

Keyboard Shortcuts and Gestures

Keyboard shortcuts and gestures can dramatically improve productivity by reducing the need to navigate menus.

1. **Common Keyboard Shortcuts**:

   ○ **Taking Screenshots**:
      - Full screen: **Ctrl + Show Windows key**
      - Partial screen: **Ctrl + Shift + Show Windows key**, then select the desired area.
   ○ **Opening Apps and Tools**:
      - Open the app launcher: **Search (Launcher) key**.
      - Open the Files app: **Alt + Shift + M**.

- ○ **Navigating Chrome Tabs**:
    - ■ Switch between tabs: **Ctrl + Tab** or **Ctrl + Shift + Tab**.
    - ■ Reopen a closed tab: **Ctrl + Shift + T**.
- ○ **System Controls**:
    - ■ Adjust brightness: Use the brightness keys on the keyboard.
    - ■ Adjust volume: Use the volume keys or **Alt + Volume Up/Down**.

2. **Touchpad Gestures**:

- ○ **Scrolling**:
    - ■ Use two fingers to scroll up or down.
- ○ **Swiping Between Tabs**:
    - ■ Swipe left or right with three fingers to switch tabs in Chrome.
- ○ **Viewing Open Windows**:
    - ■ Swipe down with three fingers to open the Overview

mode and see all open
windows.

- o **Right-click**:
  - ■ Tap with two fingers or press
    Alt and click.

3. **Touchscreen Gestures (If Applicable)**:

- o **Pinch to Zoom**: Use two fingers to
  zoom in or out on the screen.
- o **Swiping Up**: Access the app
  launcher by swiping up from the
  bottom.
- o **Swiping Between Desks**: Swipe
  left or right with three fingers to
  switch between virtual desktops.

4. **Learning More Shortcuts**:

- o Press **Ctrl + Alt + ?** to view a
  complete on-screen map of
  Chromebook shortcuts.

Maintaining and Troubleshooting Your Chromebook

Proper maintenance and troubleshooting practices ensure that your Chromebook operates smoothly and remains reliable for everyday use. This section provides comprehensive guidance on keeping your Chromebook updated, diagnosing and resolving issues, resetting the device when necessary, and seeking additional help when needed.

Updating ChromeOS

Regular updates to ChromeOS ensure your Chromebook stays secure, functional, and compatible with new features.

1. **Why Updates Matter**:

   o Updates provide the latest security patches, bug fixes, and new features, ensuring optimal performance and protection against vulnerabilities.
   o ChromeOS updates occur automatically in the background, requiring minimal user intervention.

2. **Manually Checking for Updates**:

   o Open **Settings** by clicking the clock in the bottom-right corner and selecting the gear icon.
   o Navigate to **About ChromeOS** at the bottom of the menu.
   o Click **Check for updates** to see if a new update is available.

- If an update is found, it will download automatically. Restart your Chromebook to complete the installation.

3. **Troubleshooting Update Issues**:

- Ensure your Chromebook is connected to a stable internet connection.
- Free up storage space if updates fail due to insufficient space.
- If an update doesn't complete, restart your device and try again.

4. **Update Frequency**:

- ChromeOS updates are rolled out approximately every 4–6 weeks.
- Devices eventually reach an **Auto Update Expiration (AUE)** date, after which they no longer receive updates. Check your Chromebook's AUE in **Settings > About ChromeOS > Additional details**.

Diagnosing and Fixing Common Issues

Even the most reliable devices can encounter problems. Knowing how to identify and address issues quickly can save time and frustration.

1. **Performance Issues**:

    ○ **Slow Performance**:
        - Close unnecessary tabs and apps to free up system resources.
        - Clear your browser cache and cookies: **Settings > Privacy and security > Clear browsing data**.
        - Restart your Chromebook to refresh the system.
    ○ **Low Storage**:
        - Use the Files app to delete unused files.
        - Move large files to Google Drive or an external drive.

2. **Internet Connectivity Problems**:

   o **Wi-Fi Not Connecting**:
   - Restart your Chromebook and router.
   - Forget the Wi-Fi network and reconnect by entering the password again: **Settings > Network > Wi-Fi > Forget**.
   o **Ethernet Issues**:
   - Ensure the cable is securely connected. Test with another device or cable to verify the issue.

3. **App Crashes or Unresponsiveness**:

   o Update the app through the Google Play Store.
   o Force stop and restart the app: Open **Settings > Apps > Manage apps**, select the app, and click **Force stop**.
   o Uninstall and reinstall the app if the problem persists.

4. Hardware Problems:

- **Keyboard or Touchpad Not Working**:
  - Restart your Chromebook.
  - Check for debris under the keys or on the touchpad.
- **Screen Flickering**:
  - Update ChromeOS to ensure compatibility with display drivers.
  - Adjust display settings: **Settings > Device > Displays**.
- **Battery Not Charging**:
  - Check the power adapter and cable for damage.
  - Ensure the charging port is clean and unobstructed.

5. Audio Issues:

- Check volume levels and mute settings.

- ○ Test with different audio devices or headphones.
- ○ Restart your Chromebook if the problem persists.

Factory Reset and Powerwash

A factory reset, or Powerwash, is a last-resort solution to resolve persistent issues or prepare your device for a new user.

1. **When to Use Powerwash**:

   - ○ To address severe performance issues, software glitches, or malware.
   - ○ To wipe your device clean before selling or gifting it.

2. **How to Perform a Powerwash**:

   - ○ Back up important files to Google Drive or an external device.

- ○ Open **Settings** > **Advanced** > **Reset settings**.
- ○ Click **Reset** next to **Powerwash**, then follow the on-screen instructions.
- ○ Your Chromebook will restart and return to its factory settings.

3. **Post-Reset Setup**:

- ○ Reconnect to Wi-Fi and sign in with your Google account.
- ○ Reinstall necessary apps and restore files from your backup.

4. **Alternative Hard Reset**:

- ○ If the device is unresponsive, hold down **Refresh** and tap **Power** to restart. For devices with a removable battery, disconnect and reconnect the battery.

Contacting Support

When troubleshooting on your own isn't enough, reaching out to Chromebook support channels can help resolve more complex issues.

1. **Using Built-in Help**:

   - Open the **Explore** app (found in the app launcher) for guided tutorials and troubleshooting tips.
   - Type your issue in the **Search bar** to access relevant resources.

2. **Google Support**:

   - Visit the Google Chromebook Help Center for detailed guides, FAQs, and contact options.
   - Use the **Contact Us** feature on the Help Center to connect with support via chat, email, or phone.

3. **Manufacturer Support**:

   - For hardware-specific issues, contact the manufacturer of your Chromebook (e.g., Acer, ASUS,

HP, Dell). Check the warranty status for repair or replacement options.

4. **Community Forums**:

   ○ Join forums like the **Google Chromebook Community** to ask questions and find solutions shared by other users.

5. **In-person Support**:

   ○ Visit authorized service centers or tech retailers for professional diagnosis and repair.

Security and Privacy on Chromebook

Chromebooks are designed with security and privacy in mind, making them one of the safest computing devices available. From built-in safeguards to customizable settings, Chromebooks offer tools to protect your data and ensure your online activity remains private.

Enabling Two-Factor Authentication

Two-Factor Authentication (2FA) adds an extra layer of security to your Google account, ensuring that even if someone has your password, they can't access your account without a second form of verification.

1. **What Is Two-Factor Authentication?**

    o 2FA requires you to verify your identity using two methods: your password and a secondary factor, such as a code sent to your phone.
    o This significantly reduces the risk of unauthorized access, even if your password is compromised.

2. **Setting Up 2FA on Your Google Account**:

    o Open your Google Account at https://myaccount.google.com.
    o Go to **Security** > **2-Step Verification** and click **Get Started**.
    o Choose your second verification method:
       ▪ **Google Prompt**: Receive a prompt on a connected device to confirm your login.

- ■ **Text Message or Call**: Get a one-time code via SMS or phone call.
- ■ **Authenticator App**: Use apps like Google Authenticator or Authy to generate time-based codes.
- ■ **Security Key**: Use a physical USB or Bluetooth security key for authentication.

3. **Backup Options**:

   ○ Set up backup methods like printable codes or an alternative phone number in case you lose access to your primary method.

4. **Using 2FA with ChromeOS**:

   ○ Once 2FA is enabled, you'll be prompted to complete the second verification step when signing into your Chromebook.

Managing Passwords with Chrome

Managing passwords securely is crucial for maintaining your online safety. Chrome provides an integrated password manager to simplify this process.

1. **Chrome's Built-in Password Manager**:

   - Automatically saves and fills passwords for websites and apps.
   - Generates strong, unique passwords for new accounts.

2. **Accessing Saved Passwords**:

   - Open Chrome and go to **Settings** > **Autofill** > **Passwords**.
   - View, edit, or delete saved passwords by clicking the eye icon (you'll need to enter your Google account credentials).

3. **Enabling Password Checkup**:

- o Chrome automatically checks your saved passwords against known data breaches.
- o If compromised passwords are detected, you'll receive recommendations to change them.

4. **Tips for Strong Password Management**:

- o Use unique passwords for each account.
- o Combine uppercase and lowercase letters, numbers, and special characters.
- o Avoid using easily guessable information like birthdays or common words.

5. **Using Third-Party Password Managers**:

- o For additional features, consider apps like LastPass, 1Password, or Dashlane, which are compatible with ChromeOS.

Understanding Chromebook's Built-in Security

Chromebooks are designed with multiple layers of security to protect users from malware, unauthorized access, and data loss.

1. **Verified Boot**:

   o Every time your Chromebook starts, it performs a self-check to ensure the operating system hasn't been tampered with. If a problem is detected, the system automatically repairs itself.

2. **Sandboxing**:

   o Each tab and app runs in its own isolated environment, preventing malicious code from spreading to other parts of the system.

3. **Automatic Updates**:

   o ChromeOS updates itself in the background, ensuring you always

have the latest security patches
without manual intervention.

4. **Data Encryption**:

   o All user data on a Chromebook is
   encrypted using tamper-resistant
   hardware. Even if the device is lost
   or stolen, the data is nearly
   impossible to access without your
   credentials.

5. **Guest Mode and User Accounts**:

   o Use **Guest Mode** for temporary
   users to prevent access to your files
   and settings.
   o Protect your account with a strong
   password or PIN.

6. **Powerwash for Data Reset**:

   o If your Chromebook is
   compromised, you can perform a
   Powerwash to reset it to factory
   settings, wiping all data from the
   device.

Using VPNs on ChromeOS

A Virtual Private Network (VPN) encrypts your internet connection, hiding your activity from hackers, ISPs, and even government surveillance.

1. **Why Use a VPN?**

   o Protect your online privacy and prevent tracking.
   o Access content restricted by region (e.g., streaming services).
   o Secure your connection when using public Wi-Fi networks.

2. **Setting Up a VPN on Chromebook:**

   o **Built-in VPN Support:**
     ■ ChromeOS supports OpenVPN, L2TP/IPsec, and third-party VPN apps.
   o **Using Chrome Web Store Extensions:**

- Install a VPN extension like NordVPN, ExpressVPN, or Surfshark directly from the Chrome Web Store.
  - **Using Android VPN Apps**:
    - Install a VPN app from the Google Play Store, log in, and activate it.
  - **Manually Adding a VPN**:
    - Go to **Settings** > **Network** > **Add connection** > **Add VPN**. Enter the VPN provider's server and login details.

3. **Best Practices for VPN Use**:

   - Choose a reputable VPN provider with a no-logs policy.
   - Verify that the VPN encrypts traffic and doesn't significantly reduce internet speed.
   - Regularly update the VPN app or extension for improved security.

4. Limitations of VPNs:

○ A VPN can't protect you from phishing attacks or malware, so always practice safe browsing habits.

Advanced Features and Tips

Chromebooks are simple on the surface but offer powerful advanced features and customizations for users who want to unlock their full potential. This section explores how to run Linux apps, use ChromeOS Developer Mode, master keyboard shortcuts, and optimize battery life.

Running Linux Apps on Chromebook

Running Linux apps on a Chromebook can greatly expand its functionality, allowing you to use a wide range of software not available on ChromeOS or Android.

1. **Why Use Linux Apps?**

   o Access powerful tools for
     programming, development,
     graphic design, and more.
   o Run desktop-class applications like
     GIMP (image editing), LibreOffice
     (productivity suite), and VLC
     (media player).

2. **Enabling Linux (Beta)**:

   o Open **Settings** on your
     Chromebook.
   o Navigate to **Developers** (under
     Advanced in some devices).
   o Click **Turn On** next to **Linux
     Development Environment
     (Beta)**.
   o Follow the on-screen instructions to
     set up Linux, including creating a
     username and allocating storage.

3. **Installing and Using Linux Apps**:

- ○ Open the **Terminal** from your app launcher.
- ○ Use the sudo apt-get install [app-name] command to install apps (e.g., sudo apt-get install gimp).
- ○ Launch installed apps from the Linux folder in your app launcher.

4. **Managing Linux Storage and Performance**:

- ○ Adjust Linux storage settings in **Settings > Developers > Linux**.
- ○ Keep Linux apps and packages updated using sudo apt-get update && sudo apt-get upgrade.

5. **Troubleshooting Linux on Chromebook**:

- ○ If Linux apps crash or behave erratically, restart the Linux environment or reinstall the app.

   ○ For advanced debugging, check error logs using the dmesg or journalctl commands.

Using ChromeOS Developer Mode

ChromeOS Developer Mode provides access to advanced features and customization options, including the ability to install third-party operating systems or software.

1. **What Is Developer Mode?**

   ○ A special mode that removes some of ChromeOS's restrictions, allowing deeper access to the system.

   ○ Ideal for tech-savvy users or developers looking to explore beyond ChromeOS's default capabilities.

2. **Enabling Developer Mode**:

○ Turn off your Chromebook and
press **Esc + Refresh + Power** to
boot into Recovery Mode.
○ When the recovery screen appears,
press **Ctrl + D**, then press **Enter** to
confirm.
○ Your Chromebook will reset, and
Developer Mode will be enabled
after a restart.

3. **Features of Developer Mode**:

○ Install custom operating systems or
software.
○ Access system files and developer
tools.
○ Enable SSH servers and set up
more advanced Linux
configurations.

4. **Cautions When Using Developer Mode**:

○ **Security Risks**: Developer Mode
disables Verified Boot, making the
system more vulnerable.

○ **Data Loss**: Enabling Developer Mode wipes all local data. Back up your files first.

○ **Warranty Implications**: Some manufacturers may void the warranty if Developer Mode causes damage.

5. **Exiting Developer Mode**:

○ To disable Developer Mode, restart your Chromebook and follow the on-screen instructions to restore default settings.

Chromebook Keyboard Tricks

Mastering Chromebook keyboard shortcuts can boost productivity and make everyday tasks faster and more efficient.

1. **Essential Shortcuts**:

- ○ **Search apps and files**: Press the **Launcher key** (🔍 or ⊞).
- ○ **Take a screenshot**: Press **Ctrl + Show Windows** (a rectangle with two vertical lines).
- ○ **Open a new tab in Chrome**: Press **Ctrl + T**.
- ○ **Switch between open windows**: Press **Alt + Tab**.

2. **Advanced Shortcuts**:

- ○ **Split screen**: Press **Alt + [** or **Alt +]** to snap a window to the left or right of the screen.
- ○ **Show all shortcuts**: Press **Ctrl + Alt + /** to view a complete list of keyboard shortcuts.
- ○ **Reopen closed tabs**: Press **Ctrl + Shift + T**.
- ○ **Zoom in or out**: Press **Ctrl + +** or **Ctrl + -**.

3. **Customizing Keyboard Settings**:

○ Open **Settings** > **Device** > **Keyboard**.

○ Remap keys like **Search**, **Ctrl**, or **Alt** for a personalized experience.

4. **Power User Keyboard Tips**:

○ Combine shortcuts for complex tasks, such as **Ctrl + Shift + Q (twice)** to log out quickly.

○ Use the **Search + Arrow keys** to navigate apps and files more efficiently.

Saving Power and Extending Battery Life

Optimizing your Chromebook's power settings can extend its battery life and keep it running longer during work or travel.

1. **Adjusting Display Settings**:

○ Lower the screen brightness using the brightness keys or **Settings > Device > Displays**.

○ Use **Night Light** to reduce strain and save power at night.

2. **Managing Sleep and Power Options**:

○ Go to **Settings > Device > Power** to customize when the screen dims, the device sleeps, or powers off.

○ Set your Chromebook to sleep when the lid is closed to conserve energy.

3. **Optimizing App Usage**:

○ Close unused apps and browser tabs to reduce power consumption.

○ Avoid running resource-intensive Linux or Android apps when on battery power.

4. **Using Battery Saver Features**:

○ Enable **Battery Saver** mode on supported Chromebooks for automated power-saving adjustments.

- o Monitor battery usage in **Settings > Device > Power** to identify high-drain apps or processes.

5. **General Battery Care Tips**:

- o Avoid exposing your Chromebook to extreme temperatures.
- o Use the original charger to maintain battery health.
- o Charge the battery to around 50% if storing the Chromebook for an extended period.

For Students and Educators

Chromebooks are an essential tool in modern education, offering a range of features that make them ideal for both students and educators. Whether you're managing a virtual classroom, collaborating on group projects, or staying organized with assignments, this section provides a comprehensive guide to maximizing your Chromebook for academic success.

Setting Up Google Classroom

Google Classroom is a versatile platform that simplifies the management of courses, assignments, and communication between students and teachers.

1. **Getting Started with Google Classroom**:

   ○ Open Google Classroom at classroom.google.com.
   ○ Log in with a Google Workspace for Education account or a personal Google account.
   ○ Educators: Click + > **Create Class** to set up a new class.
   ○ Students: Click + > **Join Class** and enter the class code provided by your teacher.

2. **Organizing the Classroom**:

   ○ Use the **Stream** tab to share announcements and updates with the class.
   ○ The **Classwork** tab allows teachers to organize assignments, quizzes, and study materials into topic-based sections.

○ Use **People** to manage student and co-teacher participation.

3. **Submitting and Grading Assignments**:

   ○ Students can submit assignments directly through Google Classroom, often by attaching files from Google Drive or completing Google Forms.
   ○ Teachers can grade assignments, provide feedback, and return them within the platform.

4. **Integrating Third-Party Tools**:

   ○ Enhance Google Classroom with compatible apps like Kahoot, Quizizz, or Edpuzzle for interactive learning experiences.

5. **Tips for Success in Google Classroom**:

   ○ Enable notifications for new assignments and announcements.
   ○ Regularly check the **To-Do** section to keep track of upcoming tasks.

- Archive completed classes to keep the interface clean and organized.

Collaborative Learning Tools

Collaboration is a cornerstone of education, and Chromebooks make it easy to work together in real time using various tools.

1. **Google Workspace for Education**:

   - **Google Docs**: Collaboratively write and edit documents with real-time comments and suggestions.
   - **Google Slides**: Create group presentations with shared editing permissions.
   - **Google Sheets**: Collaborate on spreadsheets for data collection and analysis.
2. **Jamboard**:

- ○ A digital whiteboard tool for brainstorming, sketching, and collaborative problem-solving.
- ○ Use it during group discussions or as a shared workspace for remote learners.

3. **Zoom and Google Meet**:

- ○ Host virtual classes and group study sessions.
- ○ Use features like breakout rooms for smaller discussions or team-based learning.

4. **Padlet**:

- ○ A user-friendly platform for collaborative idea-sharing and multimedia posts.
- ○ Create interactive boards where students can contribute text, images, and links.

5. **Tips for Effective Collaboration**:

○ Establish clear roles and responsibilities for group projects.
○ Use shared Google Drive folders to centralize materials.
○ Communicate regularly through Google Chat or other messaging tools.

Note-Taking Apps and Study Aids

Effective note-taking and study aids can help students stay organized and excel academically.

1. **Best Note-Taking Apps**:

   ○ **Google Keep**: A minimalist tool for quick notes, to-do lists, and reminders.
   ○ **Evernote**: Ideal for organizing notes, images, and PDFs in a structured format.

○ **Microsoft OneNote**: A feature-rich app with options for handwritten notes, sketches, and multimedia.

2. **Study Aids for Chromebook**:

○ **Quizlet**: Create flashcards and study sets for self-paced learning.
○ **Khan Academy**: Access free lessons, quizzes, and interactive exercises across various subjects.
○ **Forest**: A focus app that helps students stay on task by growing virtual trees during focused study sessions.

3. **Using Chrome Extensions for Notes and Productivity**:

○ **Grammarly**: Improve writing by checking grammar and style in real time.
○ **Save to Google Drive**: Quickly save web content for later reference.

- ○ **Loom**: Record screen videos to capture lessons or presentations for review.

4. **Tips for Effective Note-Taking**:

- ○ Organize notes by subject and date using folders in Google Drive.
- ○ Use color coding or tags for easy retrieval.
- ○ Review and summarize notes regularly to reinforce learning.

Managing Assignments and Deadlines

Staying on top of assignments and deadlines is critical for academic success. Chromebooks provide a range of tools to help students and educators stay organized.

1. **Using Google Calendar**:

- Sync assignments and class schedules with Google Calendar for automatic reminders.
- Set recurring events for regular study sessions or classes.
- Share calendars with classmates or team members to coordinate group activities.

2. **Google Tasks**:

- Use Google Tasks to create to-do lists for assignments, projects, and exams.
- Set deadlines and prioritize tasks based on urgency.
- Access tasks directly from Gmail, Google Calendar, or the app launcher.

3. **Dedicated Assignment Management Apps**:

- **My Study Life**: Organize timetables, tasks, and exams in one platform.

- Todoist: A versatile task manager that integrates with Google Calendar.
- Notion: A customizable workspace for tracking assignments, creating study plans, and organizing notes.

4. **Staying Organized in Google Classroom**:

- Use the **To-Do** and **Calendar** features in Google Classroom to view all assignments and deadlines at a glance.
- Submit assignments early to avoid last-minute technical issues.

5. **Tips for Staying on Track**:

- Break down large projects into smaller, manageable tasks.
- Review deadlines weekly to adjust priorities.
- Use reminders and alarms to stay ahead of deadlines.

Ultimate Chromebook Bible

For Business and Professionals

Chromebooks have become an excellent choice for business professionals due to their portability, ease of use, security features, and integration with productivity tools. This section explores how to optimize a Chromebook for remote work, use Microsoft Office, create video content for marketing, and connect to corporate networks.

Chromebook for Remote Work

Remote work has surged in popularity, and Chromebooks are uniquely suited to meet the challenges of a remote workforce.

1. **Advantages of Chromebooks for Remote Work**:

   - **Portability**: Lightweight and long battery life make them perfect for working from anywhere.
   - **Security**: Built-in virus protection, sandboxing, and frequent updates protect sensitive work data.
   - **Collaboration**: Seamless integration with Google Workspace for real-time teamwork.

2. **Setting Up a Remote Work Environment**:

   - **Google Workspace**: Use Google Docs, Sheets, and Slides for document creation and collaboration.

- ○ **Video Conferencing**: Install apps like Zoom, Google Meet, or Microsoft Teams for virtual meetings.
- ○ **Cloud Storage**: Leverage Google Drive or other cloud services like Dropbox for file access across devices.

3. **Tips for Staying Productive**:

- ○ **Use Virtual Desks**: Organize workspaces for different projects to stay focused.
- ○ **Enable Offline Mode**: Access Gmail, Google Docs, and other apps without internet to continue working during outages.
- ○ **Keyboard Shortcuts**: Learn productivity-enhancing shortcuts to streamline tasks.

4. **Remote Work Security**:

- Use **VPNs** to secure connections when accessing corporate resources.
- Store files on cloud platforms instead of local drives to ensure secure backups.
- Enable two-factor authentication (2FA) for additional protection on work accounts.

Using Microsoft Office on Chromebook

Many professionals rely on Microsoft Office for productivity, and Chromebooks support this suite through web and Android apps.

1. **Options for Accessing Microsoft Office**:

   - **Office Web Apps**: Use Word, Excel, and PowerPoint online at office.com.
   - **Microsoft 365 Subscription**: Access premium features through a

subscription, either via the web or Android apps.

- **Install Android Apps**: Download Office apps like Word, Excel, and PowerPoint from the Google Play Store for offline use.

2. **Working with Office Files on Chromebook**:

- Open Office files directly in the corresponding web or Android app.
- Use **Google Drive** to store and convert Office documents if needed.
- Enable the **Office Editing for Docs, Sheets, and Slides** Chrome extension to edit Office files directly in Google Workspace apps.

3. **Integrating Office with Google Workspace**:

- Sync files between Google Drive and OneDrive for unified access.

- Collaborate on documents by exporting Office files to Google formats or vice versa.

4. **Tips for a Seamless Experience**:

- Pin frequently used Office apps to the Chromebook Shelf for quick access.
- Enable offline mode in Office Android apps for uninterrupted work.
- Regularly update apps to ensure compatibility and performance.

Video Editing for Marketing

Marketing professionals often need to create video content for campaigns. Chromebooks offer several tools for video editing that cater to different levels of expertise.

1. **Video Editing Apps for Chromebook**:

- ○ **Clipchamp**: A web-based editor ideal for creating social media videos.
- ○ **WeVideo**: Cloud-based software with robust editing features like green screen effects and multi-track editing.
- ○ **KineMaster**: A powerful Android app with advanced editing tools and templates.

2. **Tips for Effective Video Editing**:

- ○ **Plan Your Content**: Use storyboards to map out video sequences.
- ○ **Keep It Simple**: For marketing, focus on clear messaging and visual appeal.
- ○ **Optimize for Platforms**: Export videos in formats and resolutions suited for platforms like YouTube, Instagram, or TikTok.

3. **Enhancing Video Quality**:

- o Use external microphones and webcams to improve audio and video capture.
- o Leverage stock footage and music libraries available in tools like Clipchamp.
- o Add branding elements like logos, watermarks, and consistent color themes.

4. **Sharing and Distributing Marketing Videos**:

- o Upload directly to platforms like YouTube or social media from the video editor.
- o Use Google Drive or Dropbox to share videos with team members for review and collaboration.

Connecting to Corporate Networks

Chromebooks are designed to integrate seamlessly into corporate environments, ensuring secure and efficient connectivity.

1. **Setting Up Wi-Fi and VPNs**:

   ○ Connect to corporate Wi-Fi networks using **Settings > Network > Wi-Fi**.
   ○ For secure access to internal resources, configure a **VPN**:
      ■ Use built-in ChromeOS VPN clients or third-party extensions from the Chrome Web Store.
      ■ Enter network credentials provided by your IT department.

2. **Using Virtual Desktop Infrastructure (VDI)**:

   ○ Access Windows or Linux desktops remotely through VDI solutions like **Citrix Workspace**, **VMware**

Horizon, or **Parallels Desktop** for ChromeOS.

○ Ensure you have the required permissions and software provided by your company.

3. **Accessing Shared Drives and Printers**:

○ Use **File > Add New Service** to connect to shared corporate drives.

○ Configure printers in **Settings > Devices > Printers**, entering network printer details as needed.

4. **Managing Security in Corporate Networks**:

○ Follow your company's guidelines for secure device usage, including password policies and data encryption.

○ Enable ChromeOS's **Managed Devices** settings if your Chromebook is part of a corporate fleet, allowing IT administrators to enforce policies.

5. Tips for Seamless Connectivity:

- Keep ChromeOS updated to ensure compatibility with corporate tools.
- Maintain open communication with IT support for troubleshooting and configuration.
- Use Chrome Remote Desktop to connect to office computers if needed.

Switching from Other Devices

Transitioning to a Chromebook from Windows or MacOS can feel like a significant change, but with the right guidance, the process can be smooth and rewarding. This section provides comprehensive steps to help you switch, import your files and settings, and migrate to Google services effectively.

Transitioning from Windows or MacOS

Moving from traditional operating systems like Windows or MacOS to ChromeOS requires understanding the differences and adapting to a new workflow.

1. **Understanding Key Differences**:

   o **Cloud-Centric Approach**: ChromeOS relies heavily on cloud storage, primarily Google Drive, instead of local hard drives.
   o **App Ecosystem**: ChromeOS uses web apps, Android apps from the Google Play Store, and Linux apps, rather than native Windows or Mac software.
   o **Updates and Security**: ChromeOS updates automatically in the background and has built-in security features, reducing the need for manual updates or antivirus software.

2. **Adapting to ChromeOS Features**:

○ Learn the ChromeOS **launcher** (similar to the Start Menu on Windows or Launchpad on Mac).

○ Use the **Shelf** as a customizable taskbar for frequently used apps.

○ Familiarize yourself with gestures and shortcuts for navigating the system efficiently.

3. **Preparing for the Transition**:

○ Create a Google account if you don't already have one, as it's essential for using a Chromebook.

○ Identify critical software you use on Windows or Mac and find ChromeOS-compatible alternatives (e.g., Microsoft Office 365 or Google Workspace).

○ Backup files from your old device to an external drive or cloud storage.

Importing Files and Settings

Transferring your files and settings ensures a seamless transition to your Chromebook.

1. **Backing Up Files from Your Old Device**:

   - **Windows**: Use File Explorer to copy documents, photos, and other files to an external drive or cloud storage like Google Drive or Dropbox.
   - **MacOS**: Use Finder to back up files to an external drive or iCloud. You can also use Google Drive for cross-platform accessibility.

2. **Transferring Files to Chromebook**:

   - Use an external USB drive or SD card: Insert the drive into your Chromebook and copy files using the **Files app**.
   - Upload files to **Google Drive** from your old device and access them directly on the Chromebook.

3. **Syncing Browser Data**:

   ○ Install Google Chrome on your
      Windows or Mac device.
   ○ Log in to Chrome with your Google
      account and sync bookmarks,
      passwords, and browsing history.
   ○ On your Chromebook, log in to the
      same Google account to
      automatically access synced
      browser data.

4. **Importing Photos and Media**:

   ○ Use Google Photos to back up and
      access your photos across devices.
      Install the **Google Backup and
      Sync** tool on your old device to
      upload media to Google Photos.
   ○ For videos or music files, store
      them in Google Drive or use
      external storage for transfer.

5. **Migrating Emails**:

- Set up your Gmail account to fetch emails from other accounts via POP3 or IMAP.
- If using Outlook or Apple Mail, export your emails and import them into Gmail.

Migrating to Google Services

Google's ecosystem is central to the Chromebook experience. Transitioning to Google services allows for seamless integration and better productivity.

1. **Moving from Microsoft Office to Google Workspace**:

   - Upload Word, Excel, and PowerPoint files to **Google Drive**. These files can be opened and edited in Google Docs, Sheets, and Slides, respectively.

- ○ Use the **Office Editing for Docs, Sheets, and Slides** extension in Chrome to edit Office files without conversion.
- ○ Export Google Docs, Sheets, or Slides files back to Office formats if needed for compatibility.

2. **Replacing Desktop Applications**:

- ○ Replace **Microsoft Outlook** with Gmail or the Gmail app for email.
- ○ Use Google Calendar to manage appointments and events.
- ○ Switch from OneDrive or iCloud to Google Drive for file storage.

3. **Syncing Contacts and Calendars**:

- ○ Import contacts to Google Contacts from Outlook, Apple Contacts, or other sources.
- ○ Export calendars from Apple Calendar or Microsoft Outlook and import them into Google Calendar.

4. Migrating Photos and Media Libraries:

- Install **Google Photos** on your old device to upload photos and videos. These will be accessible on your Chromebook through the Photos app or Google Drive.
- For music, use streaming services like YouTube Music or Spotify, as Chromebooks are designed to work with cloud-based media.

5. Adopting Google Productivity Tools:

- **Google Keep**: Replace desktop note-taking apps like Sticky Notes or Apple Notes.
- **Google Tasks**: Organize your to-do lists and integrate them with Google Calendar.
- **Google Maps**: Use web or app versions for navigation and location management.

Tips for a Smooth Transition

1. **Take Advantage of Built-in Tutorials**:

   o Chromebooks feature an onboarding tutorial that introduces key features and shortcuts.

2. **Experiment with Android and Linux Apps**:

   o Install Android apps for added functionality, such as Microsoft Office or Adobe Lightroom.
   o Explore Linux apps for advanced software needs, like coding or professional design tools.

3. **Leverage the Cloud**:

   o Shift your workflow to cloud-based apps to ensure accessibility across devices.

4. **Give Yourself Time to Adjust**:

- ○ ChromeOS may feel unfamiliar initially, but its simplicity will become intuitive with regular use.

FAQs and Troubleshooting Scenarios

This section addresses some of the most common questions and issues Chromebook users encounter, along with practical tips to enhance your experience. Whether you're a new user or a seasoned pro, these FAQs and troubleshooting scenarios can help you maximize the potential of your Chromebook.

Quick Fixes for Common Problems

1. My Chromebook Won't Turn On

- ○ **Check Power**: Ensure the Chromebook is plugged in and charging. Look for the charging light indicator.
- ○ **Hard Reset**: Hold down the Refresh key and tap the Power button. Release the Refresh key when the Chromebook starts.
- ○ **Battery Check**: If the device still doesn't start, let it charge for at least 15 minutes before attempting again.

2. Wi-Fi Won't Connect

- ○ **Reconnect to Network**: Go to **Settings > Network** and forget the Wi-Fi network. Reconnect by entering the password.
- ○ **Restart Modem/Router**: Restart your internet equipment to refresh the connection.

- ○ **Check Network Settings**: Ensure your Chromebook's network settings match your router configuration (e.g., 2.4 GHz vs. 5 GHz).

3. **Chromebook is Running Slowly**

- ○ **Close Tabs and Apps**: Too many open tabs or apps can slow down performance. Close unused ones.
- ○ **Clear Cache and Cookies**: Go to **Settings > Privacy and Security > Clear Browsing Data** to remove temporary files.
- ○ **Check Extensions**: Disable unnecessary Chrome extensions via **Settings > Extensions**.

4. **The Screen is Frozen**

- ○ **Force Restart**: Hold the Power button for 10 seconds until the device shuts down. Restart normally.

- ○ **Hard Reset**: Use the Refresh + Power key combination to restart the system.

5. **External Device Isn't Working**

   - ○ **Check Compatibility**: Ensure the device (USB, printer, etc.) is compatible with ChromeOS.
   - ○ **Restart Chromebook**: Unplug the device, restart the Chromebook, and reconnect.
   - ○ **Update ChromeOS**: Go to **Settings > About ChromeOS > Check for Updates** to ensure the latest drivers are installed.

Answers to Frequently Asked Questions

1. **Can I Use a Chromebook Without Internet?**
   Yes. Many apps, like Google Docs, Gmail, and Google Drive, offer offline functionality. Enable offline mode in

Settings for these apps.

2. **Can I Install Microsoft Office on a Chromebook?**

   Yes. You can use Microsoft Office web apps via Office.com or install the Android apps from the Google Play Store.

3. **What Happens If I Lose My Chromebook?**

   ○ Your data is safe as it's stored in the cloud.
   ○ Log in to another Chromebook or computer to access your files and apps.
   ○ If your device is stolen, use **Find My Chromebook** to remotely disable it via your Google account.

4. **How Do I Print from My Chromebook?**

   ○ Use **Settings > Devices > Printers** to set up a network printer.

○ Alternatively, use a USB connection if the printer supports it.

5. **Can I Play Games on a Chromebook?**

   ○ Yes, you can play Android games from the Google Play Store.
   ○ For more advanced gaming, try streaming services like Nvidia GeForce Now or Xbox Cloud Gaming.

6. **How Do I Use Linux Apps on a Chromebook?**
   Enable Linux via **Settings > Developers > Linux Development Environment**. Once set up, you can install Linux apps through the terminal.

7. **Can I Run Windows Programs on a Chromebook?**
   Not natively, but you can use virtual desktop solutions like **Parallels Desktop for ChromeOS** or remote desktop apps to access a Windows environment.

8. **Is My Chromebook Secure?**

   Yes. Chromebooks are designed with built-in security features like sandboxing, verified boot, and automatic updates to protect against threats.

Tips for Getting the Most Out of Your Chromebook

1. **Master Keyboard Shortcuts**

   ○ Save time by learning shortcuts like **Ctrl + Alt + ?** to view a list of available shortcuts.

2. **Use Virtual Desks**

   ○ Organize your workflow with multiple desktops for different tasks. Access Virtual Desks via the Overview mode (**F5 key** or swipe up with three fingers on a trackpad).

3. **Enable Offline Access**

- Set up offline mode in Google Drive, Gmail, and other apps to work without internet access.

4. **Customize Your Chromebook**

- Personalize the Shelf, Quick Settings, and Wallpaper to suit your preferences.
- Use themes in the Chrome browser to enhance your browsing experience.

5. **Optimize Battery Life**

- Lower screen brightness and disable Bluetooth when not in use.
- Close unnecessary apps and tabs to reduce power consumption.

6. **Explore Extensions and Apps**

- Install Chrome extensions and Android apps to expand

functionality, from productivity tools to creative software.

7. **Take Advantage of Google Assistant**

   o Enable Google Assistant for quick access to information, reminders, and tasks.

8. **Experiment with Linux**

   o For advanced users, Linux adds powerful tools like coding environments and professional-grade software to your Chromebook.

9. **Stay Up-to-Date**

   o Regularly check for ChromeOS updates via **Settings > About ChromeOS** to access new features and security improvements.

10. **Backup Your Data**

○ Use Google Drive for automatic backups, or connect an external hard drive for local file storage.

Future of ChromeOS

ChromeOS has evolved significantly since its introduction, transforming from a simple browser-based operating system into a versatile platform for productivity, entertainment, and education. As technology continues to advance, ChromeOS is set to grow even further, with new updates and features that enhance user experiences, expand functionality, and maintain its competitive edge.

Latest Updates and Features

ChromeOS is updated frequently, with new features and improvements rolled out approximately every four weeks. Here are some of the latest innovations:

1. **Improved App Ecosystem**:

    o **Android App Integration**: Continuous improvements make Android apps run more seamlessly on ChromeOS. Enhanced touch and keyboard support allow users to enjoy apps originally designed for mobile devices.

    o **Linux on ChromeOS**: Linux support has expanded, enabling developers and power users to access advanced tools for programming, software development, and design.

2. **Enhanced Multitasking**:

    o **Virtual Desks**: The ability to create and manage multiple virtual desktops helps users organize workflows, whether for work, study, or leisure.

    o **Improved Overview Mode**: Enhanced gestures and animations make navigating between apps and desktops more intuitive.

3. **Google Assistant Integration**:

   ○ Google Assistant on ChromeOS continues to improve, offering smarter voice commands, better integration with smart home devices, and expanded support for productivity tasks like scheduling and reminders.

4. **Gaming Enhancements**:

   ○ **Steam on ChromeOS**: Select Chromebooks now support Steam gaming, bringing popular PC games to ChromeOS.

   ○ **Game Streaming Services**: Integration with platforms like Nvidia GeForce Now, Xbox Cloud Gaming, and Google Stadia (while active) enhances gaming experiences without needing high-end hardware.

5. Security and Privacy Upgrades:

- **Enhanced Sandboxing**: Each app and web page operates in its own secure environment to prevent malicious attacks.
- **Improved VPN Integration**: Support for third-party VPNs ensures secure browsing.
- **Phishing Protection**: Built-in tools warn users of suspicious websites and emails.

6. Cross-Device Sync:

- ChromeOS is increasingly integrated with Android devices, offering features like **Phone Hub** for accessing messages, notifications, and hotspot settings directly from your Chromebook.

7. Sustainability Features:

- ChromeOS devices are designed for efficiency, with updates to power

management and recyclable
hardware components.

What's Next for Chromebook Users

The future of ChromeOS is bright, with several
developments on the horizon to make
Chromebooks even more appealing:

1. **Advanced AI Integration**:

    ○ Google is likely to expand
       AI-powered features in ChromeOS,
       including smarter search tools,
       contextual recommendations, and
       AI-driven productivity aids like
       enhanced text predictions and
       image recognition.

2. **Deeper Android and Google Ecosystem
   Integration**:

    ○ Expect Chromebooks to become
       even more integrated with Android

devices, allowing seamless sharing of apps, notifications, and files across platforms. Features like **Nearby Share** will continue to evolve, enabling faster and easier file transfers.

3. **Improved Gaming Capabilities**:

   - As more Chromebooks adopt hardware optimized for gaming, including higher refresh rate displays and better graphics support, ChromeOS is poised to attract gamers who previously overlooked the platform.
   - Continued expansion of Steam and other gaming platforms on ChromeOS is anticipated.

4. **Broader App Support**:

   - Google is working to make even more Windows and Mac apps accessible through virtualization, emulation, or native compatibility layers. This will bridge the gap for professionals requiring specialized software.

5. **Customizable User Experience**:

   ○ ChromeOS may offer more personalization options, such as widget support for the desktop or an even more versatile launcher.

6. **Expanded Enterprise Features**:

   ○ With businesses increasingly adopting Chromebooks for their affordability and security, Google is expected to introduce more enterprise-grade tools like advanced VPN options, remote management systems, and productivity enhancements tailored to corporate users.

7. **Eco-Friendly Hardware and Software**:

   ○ Future Chromebooks may feature more eco-friendly materials and power-efficient processors, aligning with sustainability goals. Software updates will focus on reducing energy consumption and extending battery life.

Staying Updated on ChromeOS Developments

To stay ahead and make the most of new features and updates, Chromebook users can take several proactive steps:

1. **Enable Automatic Updates**:

   o ChromeOS updates automatically, but you can manually check for updates by going to **Settings > About ChromeOS > Check for Updates**.

2. **Follow Google's Announcements**:

○ Keep an eye on announcements
from Google I/O, where major
ChromeOS updates and features are
often revealed.

3. **Join Beta Channels**:

○ Advanced users can switch to the
Beta or **Dev** channels in ChromeOS
settings to test new features before
they are released to the public. Note
that these channels may include
bugs or unfinished features.

4. **Explore Online Communities**:

○ Forums like Reddit's **r/ChromeOS**
and the **Chromebook Help
Community** provide insights, tips,
and updates from other users and
experts.

5. **Follow Technology News Outlets**:

○ Websites like Android Central,
9to5Google, and Chrome Unboxed

regularly cover ChromeOS updates and developments.

6. **Sign Up for Newsletters**:

   ○ Subscribe to newsletters from ChromeOS-focused blogs and websites to receive regular updates directly in your inbox.

7. **Experiment with New Features**:

   ○ When updates are available, take the time to explore and experiment with new features. Many updates include subtle improvements that may enhance your experience.

Resources and Appendices

Useful Websites and Communities

1. **Official Resources**:

   ○ **Google Chromebook Help Center**:
     support.google.com/chromebook
     Your first stop for troubleshooting, guides, and FAQs provided directly by Google.
   ○ **Chromebook Official Blog**:

     blog.google/products/chromebooks/

Stay informed about the latest updates, features, and news from Google.

2. **User Communities**:

   ○ **Reddit: r/ChromeOS**:
     reddit.com/r/ChromeOS
     A vibrant community where Chromebook users share tips, ask questions, and discuss ChromeOS developments.

   ○ **Chromebook Forums**:
     community.gophermods.com
     A community-driven forum with expert advice, reviews, and troubleshooting tips.

3. **News and Review Sites**:

   ○ **Chrome Unboxed**:
     chromeunboxed.com
     Dedicated to ChromeOS news, product reviews, and tips for getting the most out of your Chromebook.

- ○ **Android Central**:
  androidcentral.com
  Offers ChromeOS-related articles,
  tutorials, and device comparisons.
4. **Education Resources**:

- ○ **Google for Education**:
  edu.google.com/chromebooks/
  A hub for educators and students to
  learn about using Chromebooks in
  academic environments.
5. **Tutorial and Video Guides**:

- ○ **YouTube Channels**:
  - ■ **Tech With Brett**: Focuses on
    ChromeOS tutorials and tips.
  - ■ **Chrome Unboxed
    (YouTube)**: Features in-depth
    reviews and hands-on guides
    for Chromebook users.

Keyboard Shortcuts Reference Guide

Mastering keyboard shortcuts can make your Chromebook experience more efficient. Here's a list of essential shortcuts:

1. **Navigation**:

   - **Open Task Manager**: Search + Esc
   - **Open Files App**: Alt + Shift + M
   - **Switch Between Open Windows**: Alt + Tab
   - **Toggle Full-Screen Mode**: F4 (or Search + F)

2. **System Controls**:

   - **Take a Screenshot**: Ctrl + Show Windows
   - **Take a Partial Screenshot**: Ctrl + Shift + Show Windows
   - **Lock Screen**: Search + L
   - **Open Settings**: Alt + Shift + S

3. **Text and Editing**:

   - **Select All**: Ctrl + A
   - **Copy**: Ctrl + C

- **Paste**: Ctrl + V
- **Undo/Redo**: Ctrl + Z / Ctrl + Shift + Z

4. Browser Shortcuts:

- **Open New Tab**: Ctrl + T
- **Reopen Closed Tab**: Ctrl + Shift + T
- **Open History**: Ctrl + H
- **Zoom In/Out**: Ctrl + Plus / Ctrl + Minus

5. Special Shortcuts:

- **View All Shortcuts**: Ctrl + Alt + ?
- **Open Quick Settings Menu**: Alt + Shift + N
- **Cycle Through Virtual Desks**: Search + [ ]

Glossary of Chromebook Terms

1. ChromeOS:

The operating system that powers

Chromebooks. It is cloud-based and lightweight, designed primarily for web applications and Android apps.

2. **Launcher**:
   The search bar and app organizer on ChromeOS, accessible via the Search key or the Shelf.

3. **Shelf**:
   The bar at the bottom of the screen (or side, depending on your settings) where pinned apps, the app launcher, and system tray are located.

4. **Virtual Desks**:
   ChromeOS's multitasking feature that lets you create and switch between multiple desktop spaces.

5. **Files App**:
   The built-in file manager in ChromeOS for accessing local, cloud, and external

storage.

6. **Google Play Store**:
   The marketplace for downloading and
   installing Android apps on a Chromebook.

7. **Linux (Beta)**:
   A feature that allows users to run Linux
   applications on ChromeOS, catering to
   developers and advanced users.

8. **Powerwash**:
   A factory reset feature that restores your
   Chromebook to its original state.

9. **Google Workspace**:
   A suite of productivity tools, including
   Google Docs, Sheets, Slides, and Gmail,
   designed for collaboration and
   cloud-based work.

10. **Phone Hub**:
    A feature that syncs your Android phone
    with your Chromebook, allowing you to

view notifications, messages, and more.

11. **Sandboxing**:
A security feature that isolates apps and web pages to prevent malware or other threats from affecting your Chromebook.

12. **PWA (Progressive Web App)**:
A web-based application that works like a native app, providing offline access and better performance compared to regular web pages.

13. **Show Windows Key**:
A function key (usually represented as a rectangle with two vertical lines) used for multitasking, such as taking screenshots or switching apps.

14. **Quick Settings**:
A panel in the bottom-right corner of the Shelf that provides access to essential system controls like Wi-Fi, Bluetooth, and

volume.

15.   **Verified Boot**:

A security feature that ensures the integrity of ChromeOS during startup. If tampering is detected, the system will revert to a safe state.

Ultimate Chromebook Bible

Ultimate Chromebook Bible